FREE CLEAN FILL DIRT

AKRON SERIES IN POETRY

FREE CLEAN FILL DIRT

CARYL PAGEL

 The University of Akron Press
Akron, Ohio

ISBN: 978-1-62922-033-8 (paper)
ISBN: 978-1-62922-146-5 (ePDF)
ISBN: 978-1-62922-147-2 (ePub)

A catalog record for this title is available from the Library of Congress.

∞ The paper used in this publication meets the minimum requirements of ANSI/NISO Z39.48–1992
(Permanence of Paper).

Cover image: "Fall Nocturne," 2015, by Ron Barron. Used with permission. Cover design by Amy Freels.

Free Clean Fill Dirt was designed and typeset in Garamond with Montserrat titles by Amy Freels and
printed on sixty-pound white and bound by Baker & Taylor Publisher Services of Ashland, Ohio.

Produced in conjunction with the University

of Akron Affordable Learning Initiative.
More information is available at
www.uakron.edu/affordablelearning/

For Oily Doily, Garden Party, Excisions, and Aye Aye

CONTENTS

In every part of every living thing
is stuff that once was rock

—Lorine Niedecker

I suppose you suppose that yon of little burial
Is non of? Rather it is of universal o'er.
Unvast because it unvast looks?
Well, how wrong sir.

—Russell Atkins

SEVERANCE CENTER

Is that part

of the stem—the

one that bends—

around the pole—stood

there now decades

ago—the stem that

mended obstruction by

humbly *arounding*—shooting through

it—is it

then—that stem—*evidence*—

of memory or

an antenna?   Alien force

for sure tasked

to twist about the

ruin of what's

been reckless (this city's

past's past's making)—

growth a mark of

unreasonable season—growth

showing where a wild

coyote walked kingly

down the street at

dawn   No   Wait

wild is wrong   You

didn't see it

There can't be any

longer wild   Wild

is the one that

lives inside watching

from the window what

is wilder still

than him—with vigilance

You touch him

thinking most creatures can't

believe can't recall

their own beginning   Ends

we witness—but

that stem started long

before you thought

to meet it—and

around it bends—

born in cement   Have

you put a

face to your enemy?

Have you sat

in séance?   Have you

asked your dead

what way yet?   Have

you finished accounting?

Will you pack your

belongings?   Would you

ever even do that?

What would you

do?   H.D. said "we

look through a

window into the world

of pure over-mind"

and—like a cap—

it shadows us

It keeps us—so

she said—connected

to a deep internal

discerning consciousness   A

seawall—underwater lens it

rests over perception

like a jellyfish   Veil

or vision molten

blurring of the external

world in service

of something undeclared   Dense

prediction   Too too

far withdrawn to convey

that the conventional

means of making is

taking   Are you

inside or outside?   Tenacious

or troubling?   Outside

today not far away—

further violence   The

text says stay away

Don't congregate   Do

not fight but dread

cocoons—dread weaponizes

context   So you ask

your map—the

alphabet—for further instruction

An introduction   Some

pilot   A resistant direction

Are you inside

or outside?   Are you

yourself well?   What

is the memory of

a stem?   *Its*

bend   Where will you

go when you

leave here?   What has

this city's past's

past abandoned?   The gazebo

The observatory   Exhaust

You are trying to

think but *that*

sound—that sound not

strong—not a

train or a shot

Not a wail

or a clock   That

pitch   There is

something in the way

of the thought

You are revolving around

it—*stop growling*

ORDINARY STRATA (CLEVELAND)

Vacant IHOP's stripped sign more legible than it was with lights

Man sneezing into a stranger's mouth

Man returning a box of opened condoms

Man in pastel scrubs cradling his crotch at the crossing

We claim the dead branch is integral to the structure of the tree

Unscooped stoops start a parade in the streets

Tall ships come to port in June

ORDINARY STRATA (PALMER SQUARE)

Aim toward the sharpest phrase

Amidst disarray

Winter's arms wild legs akimbo squeak

Sculpture of a hand gripping the base of a tree

Poster about rats in the alley

Police won't follow up

Beetles having eaten through the bark as impetus

SATURDAY

According to the stranger

first ice sheets

will thaw sea levels

will rise you

read the stranger said

to heights unheard

of shores will smother

previous neighbors no

one will weather well

the earth's peevish

heat will increase air

itself septic streets

and bridges unbearable   Oh

the old ready

routes—the routes of

childhood—routes of

recall now a dream

unnavigable   What was

the way you once

would take to

call on the one

you loved—which

way did it begin

again it's gone—

awe intact perhaps but

face it the

stranger said we're going

to need new

ideas you read we're

going to need

new strategies tactics for

endurance   Don't ruminate

on sinkholes water supplies

toxins massive unknowable

truly undivinable fractures in

the brittle tectonic

masses   Oh delicate underworld

Oh green child

You once played orphanage

What is this

game and did you

play it?   *It's*

orphanage   You would peacefully

envision—oh grimy

child—that everyone you

knew thus far

at this small age

was dead—what's

dead—mourn your parents

sweet warm parents

taste the soil then

pretend to live

for hours on some

foggy Saturday morning

subsist on twigs carrots

chives rhubarb from

the backyard garden   Braid

a roof   You

hadn't yet read the

stranger's book—he'd

been to war—full

of dread—excitement

discerning newly revealed terrifying

conditions (or perhaps

not *new* just *said*)—

conditions of unrelenting

thirst—neighbors turning crop

shortages earthquakes storms

During those decades in

which you endured

you guess you were

a cautious person—

full of regret   Impossible

to understand   Impossible

to understand—this fact

unnatural—*unnatural* you

read the stranger wrote

but what is

natural?   He pictured all

the ways in

meditation one could end:

explosives beheading drought

gunshot lost realistic utilizations

of the imagination

for how are we

just now accepting

our trajectory as terminating

here—*breath halts*

here—it stops in

Chicago a Saturday

morning sunny bright unusually

calm so many

friends the dog snoring

at home   No

The end has already

passed   It's done

Recall a morning when

your only worry

was time (stupid)—money

(boring)—being called

another woman's name (again)

but what matters

most what matters is

not your name—

your name a tool

to test or

tell us when you've

left (not what

hurt you)   Oh silly

civic fool   Erase

it the stranger wrote

we're all already

doomed   Accept it   Dead

despite the news

of CO_2 turning to

fuel fuel turning

back despite the spiral's

whorl you drew

a long thickening tail

claiming *pineapples! constellations!*

snails!—despite Elle despite

Les despite Dad

already gone what matters

now still matters—

it matters—identify an

image or phrase—

shard of what could

bear your last

lasting thought—something durable:

the city's sirens

ice sheets rich crimson

shade of the

truck that took you

Satchel's gaze   Calm

yourself   Ask is it

simpler to accept

such fate when one

is what one

calls a woman   What

is a woman

if not skilled in

sudden cessation   Say

it: the sun isn't

getting any cooler

water cleaner   Assist each

other need new

gears visualize all impending

disasters like falling

off a building down

the stairs horrifying

a crash dementia fires

the flood food

shortages plastics cancer cancer

cancer lead…   Yes

So far it's true

you've only witnessed

one flight   You didn't

fight but felt

some I slide out

the side of

what grave scene and

if it was

replaced—that *I*—it

had a different face

ORDINARY STRATA (CLEVELAND)

Meadowbrook Road keeps the meadow's brook secret

A firetruck sale scribbled on the window in soap

Free museum

Solo tulip

Trombone player not great you heard

Man remembering his childhood in Hough

Before the hospital buildings went up

WINDOWS I

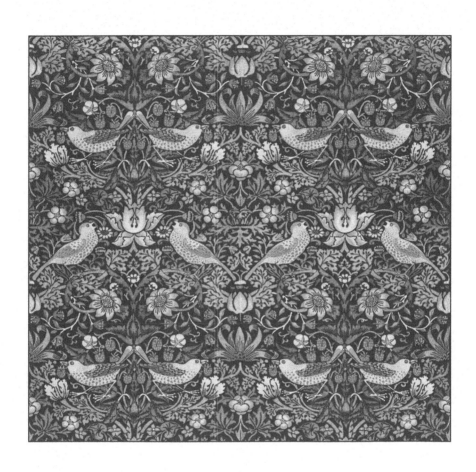

........_winter_.................'s day

Date _03 - 05 - 20_

Mood: (Happy) Sad - Tired - Quiet - Busy - Talkative

Not him/her-self

Snack: (ate) did not-tried _____

Lunch: Ate all-some-none-(most.)

Needs: _____

Activities: _ball ramp, bear push toy, activity boxes, animal sounds._

Nap: 1:00
      2:00

Toileting:

Time	BM	Wet	Toilet
9:00	✓		
12:30		✓	
3:30		✓	

THE VANITAS FLY

After Jacques Linard's A vanitas still life with a skull, an hourglass, a
tulip in a glass vase, a shell and butterfly, all resting on a stone ledge

In this version

by Jacques Linard—gouache on parchment year

undetermined—you find

a fly floating not in the Brandy

Old Fashioned (as

sometimes happens) but perched instead a fraction

of an inch

above the brow or where the painting's

skull's brow would

have been—if it still had skin—

the brow in

life no memento mori but a furrowed

field of worry—

forehead forewarning fear or focus forever performing

a kind of

counsel—as you lean in—peering closer

at the rose

tones glowing off the laptop's screen—propped

open in an

airport bar where you've lingered the last

hour browsing ancient

vanitas—temples wrinkled by attention—wrinkles evident

in this your

thirty-seventh year—on this your first anniversary—

a period in

which one might feel—from where? *inside*

or *out*?—abrupt

demand to decide what lives might alight

because of (or

not) some gut feeling   A feeling feeling

like the feeling

that in literature leads certain miserable young

men to elevate

their once friend's dead head high to

the heavens and

beg of it answers to existential questions

while for similar

reasons a woman might…what?…*drown*?…(no—

that must be

wrong)   Only clowns would activate an antidote

to abstraction by

engendering a particular alien with which to

portend—protect or

threaten (as if a baby's skull were

a crystal ball

used to foretell from the sonogram)   One

should question their

most fundamental desires   Would you call them

distraction?   Would you

say the torpid storm-worn sound-found image of

new cells forming

is vanity or vanitas?   Such crisis is

binding—it subsists

both on and inside of you   But

look: in this

version by Jacques Linard—gouache on parchment—

year undetermined—the

yellow-tipped wilting tulip shell and frozen hourglass

frame a bug

finding repose on bone—the fly's location

occasionally known as

the *third eye*—a sense of potential—

source of clairvoyance—

distinguished from but not entirely dissimilar to

the so-called *mind's*

eye—the eye with which one conceives

of scenes unscripted—

verdicts unheard yet or (in the case

of our sad

prince) deeds already done—by the ghost

of Dad—our

past's symbols acting as that which has

already been forecast

        (It's true: we've seen the play   But

        just because some

        signs are clear that doesn't mean we

        can heed them)

You lean nearer—wondering: *How many eyes*

does a fly

have?   (Refresh the tab)   *Five*   Two compound—

"ommatidium"—immobile—composed—

making panoramic mosaics of landscape—perceiving light

(the future) four

times faster than any human might   Just

try whisking such

swift pests away—their presence present as

a tickle or

itch long after wings have alit—which

is still seconds

before one's own inept hand lands—slapping

skin in what's

become the insect's ancient past—smack's sting

reiterating initial landing…

It's maddening!   One could waste a whole

day (or decade)

swatting at their torment—torment persisting whether

torment presents as

groom apparition drone or Dad—torments habitually

privileged more lines

than the minor gal—abandoned to her

rue rant ruin—

to scale the willow or perhaps—*damn*

it—deliver to

the world yet another sad sack   Best

not to dwell

on the likely paths   Instead catch cool

comfort in the

fly—an annoyance seeing nothing complete in

order to proceed

with ambition—one's future understood in shards

no harder to

hold than the entire design   The vanitas

fly sports five

eyes—two compound—three more unassuming "ocelli"

used to—so

the search says—"pinpoint its partner" but

why oh why

are we always pairing up?   Yorick's skull

returned after many

moons underground to the warm palms of

his old friends—

an enviable route you assume to resurface

as muse (amusement)

and mellow presence among one's treasured cohort

solely to provoke

another joke—for the ultimate concern on

earth (so the

skull sweetly sings two drinks in) is

not *to be*

or *not to be* (not even *who*

to make to

be) but how best to continue to

collaborate...   Oh familiar

ghosts!   We are beholden!   Yes Dad's apparition

terrified but think

of all that gossip!   Let's not look

to the wilted

princes or waterlogged women but to Yorick

for his grave

long-term pranks—jester's soil-stained charm—the alarm

he inspired in

too-serious colleagues—Oh delicate skeleton!   What ridiculous

roles we've played!

Your plane home is boarding shortly   Hear

a human's once

singular voice repeating boarding zones via mechanized

tones and consider

that every head ever rendered left to

rot or dug

up once housed its most useful tool

in the safe

soft center of itself   The tongue—muscle

tasked with stirring

speech—is still sharper than the sword

or pen—with

more precision than progeny—one's prospects more

often revealed through

talk than by any actual exacting thought

Speak to it!

urged the guards to Horatio   Say what

it is that

you really want   Make it so through

spell or oath—

tell your secrets to the nearest ghost

Graveside the gravedigger

claimed that Yorick once dumped a pitcher

of wine on

his friend's head (what fun! a baptism

if there ever

was one)—Yorick's life recalled by the

ghost king's son

with a tenderness surpassing even that expressed

for the prince's

own kin   Are we charming only in

our friend's heads?

Is delusion what eventually gets us through?

It's nine at

night   According to your ticket this will

be a short

flight   You take a quick sip from

your watery drink

and tuck a tip into the bill

book remembering that

if one hears a fly go by—

they're still alive—

remembering that you can't take any of

this with you

But what is the source of the

buzz?   How much

life is enough?   You swat at a

shadowy quiver in

the periphery of your vision—an abrupt

dim glimmer to

the side of your eye—a single

twinkling inkling at

the edge of your attention...   But there's

nothing there   No—

It's just the air   So you turn

around   You grab

your bag   You run along   You're in

such a rush

STRAW

Never have you

ever known a

more elegant tool

to suck (a

gesture already too

human)   Lips pursed

nursing pulling light

from some unseen

end of the

tunnel like a

funnel with no

waist   What waste—

this reverse gravity

strait   What minor

changes it would

take to save

us   How unwilling

we are to

make them   Our

basic instincts forecast

imminent demise: Optimism

Haste A shared

propensity for self-deception

ORDINARY STRATA (COTTAGE GROVE)

Bumps or cracks on the sycamore

The swiftest thinking about slow thought

Pushing an empty stroller home

Text making faux amends

Play the scene in your head again

Love lasts apart from action

Disregarding the way things might have been

ORDINARY STRATA (COVENTRY)

Look over by the curbside wine can

Free tree in the tree line

Pupils contract when you give up

A "window to the soul" shuts

Can we make it home before the cumulonimbi do?

Steer around a smooshed squirrel

A dearth of mentors

NOTES ON *NOTES ON THOUGHT AND VISION*

A late text

from O showing a dead whale from

the bow of

his boat bloated floating wild while O

arced the ship's

helm (you have to imagine—yourself not

a captain) *down*—

re-routing the lab's vessel *around*—to catch

a closer look

at the popping stomach—striped lurid putrid

balloon—island occupied

with gas and fat—a baffling belly

in ghastly distension

(and *yes*—you looked it up—whales

do have wombs)

at which point he framed the corpse

sans flash leaning

over to snap a pic and fire

it off—invisible

signals—only to be received by you

perched alone on

a taupe sofa at home—a home

acquired weeks before

in a gesture—so your mother joked—

that evoked optimism

by incurring debt   *True true…*   The sullen

cynical drifter in

you knows this loan tethers your soul

to a pre-owned

plot and from such soft fanned advantage

on land—podcast's

manic static masking the insistent disturbing chirping

alerting of squirrels

while you work—you tap tap tap

with your thumbs'

tips a quick note to O in

the slim space

allotted under the blue box that gifted

his missive—his

text's message (unbottled)—bubble noting that O's

assigned whale arrived

(of course) on course unbidden—soft—deceased—

in peace—causing

no harm no strain no epic chase

as demonstrated by

the phone's photo's distant pixilated image—lined

alien belly—with

pleats like those in an umbrella's bloom—

bruising pale greyish

pink—enlarged with lard—the pitiable puss

of a recently

breathless mammal having no hole or open

field in which

to steady itself and *let go* in—

though we humans

too are buried stomach up—one difference

being our eyes

face forward as if caskets have windows

while the whale

gets to point its sightless gaze downward—

into darkness—every

corpse aligned to its right night   O

wrote he wanted

to tow the bloat straight out into

the ocean in

order to unburden the bulky body's burden

of its burden

but the law pronounces whales—even lifeless—

untouchable—untouched the

mammal's required to remain until its remains

wash up on

some shore where this poor creature's fate—

like all our

fates—will depend upon the state (with

its strict systemic

rules—rules that often locate themselves ahead

of god—or

perhaps not god but *bodies*)   The state

instead will send

several men with the aid of cranes

to raise said

weight and (there is no more delicate

way to say

this) *trash it*—its matter triggering further

trouble—an outcome

entirely predictable when cleaving a corporeal performance

from its desired

course   Bewildered—entranced—stupid you reply totally

in emoji: 🐋

💀⚰️🏗️⬛   Complicit or numbed

your focus these

past few months wrecked by persistent interruption…

> *What*
>
> *is*
>
> *in*
>
> *the*
>
> *way*
>
> *of*
>
> *thought?*
>
>
> *Is*
>
> *it*
>
> *image?*

This was the end of summer—cusp

of autumn—more

than a year since   violent   disruption   resulting

in   catastrophic civic

panic   Insistent disquiet   Eradication of precision—end

of the line

So you turn to H.D. again—her

jellyfish   an emblem

of unending struggle to involve *the thought*

Lost to lost

nature—not caught—the over-mind H.D. wrote

will survive outside

of consciousness—or *above*—a trance state

pulse   as locomotion

way of retrieving clearer feeling—the jellyfish

swimming compressed opaque—

a mind physical floating through impenetrable liquid

din of primordial

    soft self   moon sea   space webbing   Lens

with which to

love   the trance state called over-mind   Brittle

        breach in surface

    vision past shape or creature   We wonder

        is it summer

forever now?   Is it the dreaded end

yet?   And if

it is the end then can we

claim we clung

to it?   The wind!   Lightning bolts flash

by   Goodbye tides!

Goodbye reefs!   Ready are you ready for

the harshest parts?

Hunger burns preventable illness opioids poverty libel—

the flu?   Preparation

paralyzed by waiting   the whale a warning

this average evening

Do you want to be of service?

Focus   The belly

gently suspended above the sea   skin   mind

your mind inside

a jellyfish able to discern storm dust—

psychic inklings—skull

inking   dripping muddy pond   bad eyes—forecast

on—this instinct

to describe what trouble   hasn't transpired yet…

Rewind rewind   (unconformity

in time)   Concentrate on where you are

and what you

are allowed to help   Concentrate on who

taught you to

want to—who provides aid   without compensation—

without expressed or

aggressive gain   who spins the gyre   Concentrate

on the current

the unspooling present thought... You're sitting on

a taupe sofa

in a grey house　　　　Satchel asleep　　　　O

on a boat—

the whale drifting away from its plotted

fate　　　We are

not safe　　　*(We are not safe)*　　　But

there is grace

(There is grace)   Our mothers are everywhere

ORDINARY STRATA (APPLEDORE ISLAND)

Golden lichen blown to the top of the radar tower

A rock talk on plastics

Gull feeding a baby to its babies

No longer antithetical no longer hypothetical

Sewing tarps on the pool table

Pulling up invertebrates with silt

Entering the shed by a door in another door

WILDERNESS

The first ship

to carry you away

wasn't named the

Martha J—which was

in fact the

ivory boat that O

would subsequently coax—

at twilight—months later—

in silence—across

the bay—to show

you seals dissolving

slowly over eroded rocks

(the engine off)

as they transitioned from

one way of

being—*breathing*—to another

Underwater the seals

unseen—immediate—attentive—present

as a mother

and then again some

days later—through

the harsh hazardous haze

of a summer

storm—you sailed out

to the Ajax

Café—that childhood haunt—

for hats and

salmon in Port Hadlock—

then back among

the blackening waves to

O's home dock

in Port Townsend   *How*

strange you might

have thought—to knot

one's lot to

a stranger's—but *maybe*

not—your stranger

stranger still since then—

just now bearing

more strata—like how

the last craft

to convey you away

was a rusty

red 1990s Bronco and

the sweet sliding

soul who one May

day decades ago

gave life to O

(years later saving

it when he wanted

out) was the

very woman the wooden

tender *Martha J*

was consequently named for

WINDOWS II

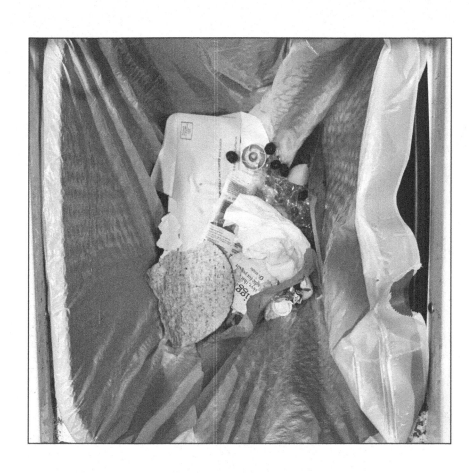

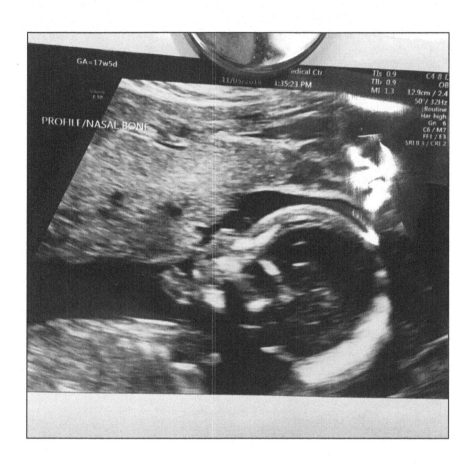

ORDINARY STRATA (CLEVELAND)

How to signal distress

An eighteenth-floor elevator opens to a waterfall

A village exists to defend where you panic

Cops under federal investigation

Two "fresh and meaty" King Babies

The toast invented as a test for poison

Our responsibility clean water

LAKEVIEW CEMETERY

Down Mayfield Road

a bit before Little

Italy—beginning at

the abandoned grade school—

ghost swings uncanny

arboreal murmurs—saddest dog

the tethered dog—

laundry line T-shirts drying

hurt squirrel shuffling

shattered legs dragging its

back half broken

across a split sidewalk—

dragging the heft

of its own infirm

frame   See versions

of this city as

it once was

over the version that

it is: abandoned

Walmart illuminated abandoned celestial

observatory abandoned clandestine

desolate country club abandoned

theater abandoned barbershop

deer coyote loose kids

a fox   Rainforest

Car Wash   Shoe and

Leather Repair   Wicked

Taco storefront closed and

then the cemetery

Who was it that

was once here—

what was it that

they did revere?

Another mile through iron

gates spring green

on Garfield's tomb—second

assassinated—interned forever

next to—*well*—his

wife   Mayors   Surgeons

Standard Oil barons   Titans

of so-called industry—

silent like there was

no omen—silent

like there is no

past   (Like memory

isn't layered—like bodies

can't corrupt)   You

heard a boy one

day darted across

a park—darted you

heard into or

through the park—his

park—not far—

his park—a boy

waving with a

boy's joy—what most

would say was

a boy's toy—playing

in a park

(his park)—near a

swing (his swings)

And who will carry

his name now?

Others still stop up

the plot: CUSHING

NESS STOKES MORGAN SHERWIN

WINTON and BRUSH

See the sign in

the gravekeeper's window

reads: FREE CLEAN FILL

DIRT   See ROCKEFELLER's

buried here   Where's TAMIR?

ORDINARY STRATA (CLEVELAND)

Syphilis is Serious billboard

Abortion is Fake Feminism billboard

Hot Sauce Williams is closing

Wicked Taco is closing

La Cave du Vin is closing

Tav Co is closed

Now it's open again in Brennan's

A HISTORY OF THE COLOR ORANGE

For Hilary Plum

Maybe orange was

born when a few twigs of tinder

were rubbed together

(at first with pleasure—a tender touch—

then later harder)

as the friction changed a soft blue

spark into white

heat—springing bright—a *flame* both warm

warning wave and

the name of the blaze's most observable

part   You predict

such primitive process probably wasn't *human improvement*

but something clarified—

made conceivable by the sight of lightning

knifing land—man

inspired to ignite by the night's ragged

light—the smoky

odor of meat steaming after a summer

storm or vision

of a paradise burning   Orange was initially

referred to as

"yellow-red" then "naranga" in Sanskrit (though "saffron"

came first) in

the early sixteenth century   It's said that

in ancient Egypt

the mineral orpiment—an orange arsenic—was

ground into pigment

and used to embellish the exteriors of

royal tombs   Orpiment

was included (along with statues pendants masks

and perfumes) in

a small paint set among the possessions

that King Tut

had stuck next to his mummified remains

for the long

and boring slog that is the voyage

to the afterlife

The powder stuck around—and orpiment could

still be found—

on the chiseled tips of arrows as

well as in

pest control   It seems even the cheeriest

natural ingredients contain

toxins—our dead less often processed as

pure compost than

imprisoned in decorative poison   Orange has always

been a warning:

think of life jackets hunter's vests highway

cones and even

the so-called safety tip of a toy

gun—a lump

of neon plastic supposed to distinguish what's

"fun" from the

real thing but (*fuck*) the real thing's

tragic deal is

that it can't be undone   Some love

orange for its

proximity to gold   Some adore it for

the color's nearness

to heat: peach campfire sun and poppy

clementine carrot parrot

and lion   We even conceive of hell

in this hue

Dante did too   Hypocrites were destined to

trudge grudgingly through

the wicked ditches of the eighth circle

of the underworld

under the eternal burden of orange cloaks

hooded and heavy

with lead lining—ordinary on the outside

but punishing within—

which makes you think of the region

where you live

Legend has it that the "Rust Belt"

was named thus

by Walter Mondale who in the early

'80s disapproved of

Reagan's breezy refusal to accept the ruin

that upset workers

residing in central states—facing downsizing after

their industry decayed—

the "rust" referring to the slow corrosion

of steel—corruption

of metal when left wet and neglected—

a picture of

perversion when a population's essentials are ignored

too long—when

the labor that's kept some people going's

gone   Rusty as

the russet flush of flowerless flower boxes—

sans beds—built

by O to bookend the draining grey

shades of your

porch—your yard—your entire town—always

down—so winter

bound   You call the six-foot brick hollows

bordering your front

door "welcome coffins"—a joke working only

on folks who

don't plan to be buried here   Orange

is the sign

of sudden detour—but also the sunny

silent pleasing tone

of robes worn by Buddhist monks—bright

like fresh egg

yolks—or the sweater of your friend

who dons amber

to many a get-together—amusing smart and

cool (she is)—

the color a contrast to the charm

of her given

name   Plum's ideal sartorial palette reminds you

of *Flaming June*—

or better yet Frida Kahlo's *Roots*—in

which the artist

reclines on her side in desert dirt—

one elbow propped

defiantly on a pillow—lime-colored ivy vines

spiraling wild through

a transparent rectangular break in her chest—

a surrealist's window—

cut open from a long orange dress

creating a shape

with which to let living material sprout

forth and nourish

the thirsty earth—her hidden heart giving

birth (or blood?)

to the sort of enduring beauty that

can't possibly hurt

anyone   There's wisdom there   Kahlo's face is

calm but *come*

on—who would prefer a ginger gown

to royal blue?

(Not you)   Frank O'Hara wrote "There should

be / so much

more, not of orange, of / words, of

how terrible orange

is / and life"   He's right   For most

of your life

you've observed bronze and tawny leaves precede

the darkest season—

a vivid spectral banner of surrender before

the impending white

cloak of cold—winter a landscape zero

(now disappearing)—but

this new year you walk instead along

a warm windy

shore in Florida—abiding with each sandy

step a heft

in your torso's window   You've been told

the algae floating

off the coast is termed "red tide"

(though it looks

more like a coral pink)—blooming pollutant—

chemicals draining into

the gulf lasting mostly only a few

weeks each season

until this year when the airborne contagion

continued for many

months causing a cold's constant cough or

constriction in some

breathers' lungs—your lungs already constricted by

no sickness but

a boy (forming) crowding organs—hoarding all

the internal real

estate   It's strange   Steel waves roar to

shore over half-moon

gaps made by your heavy heels digging

deep into weak

sand   What effort it requires to move

forward with care

What effort it requires to bear images

of Paradise burning

See the horses fleeing flaming fields in

search of a

river or less smoky spot to wait—

like the shade

of a gas station   In one picture

a donkey's secured

to a pole in the road—deer

carcasses punctuate parking

lots   You've read crabs fear wound-colored water

and sea turtles

are washing up on the coast   You

understand that this

is not a game   Having a child

will mean death

in your name   You'll be forever fated

to wear the

cloak of shame for initiating a poor

unwitting soul to

this earth's abysmal changes in an age

that likely contains

its own end   But unlike its friend

red orange doesn't

mean *stop* but *proceed with caution* and—

to be honest—

though you claim you can't imagine hell—

you don't have

to   There's proof: video of a twelve-year-old

boy being shot

in the park (it took just two

seconds—following zero

questions) by a so-called authorized adult   Watch

as the horizon

blooms honey lavender turquoise gold peach salmon

and amber   Will

this little kicking kid someday want a

gun?   What will

you do to prevent him from getting

one?   There's always

a decisive streak of neon green after

the sun's plunge

ORDINARY STRATA (LAKE ERIE)

In every living thing is stuff that now is lead

Plastics opioids pesticides estrogen

News of a stabbing in the parking lot

Unconformity or trauma in the same line

Lives are made of a few things (retold)

Dream of the taco boat

52% of men think birth control doesn't benefit them

ORDINARY STRATA (LAMBERTON ROAD)

Mushroom prints on the internet

Ad for Congress in the party lawn

Waking up early like you said you would

Burnt sweet potatoes smell

New home brew discussing its man again

Guilt for ignoring the summons stews

Winter insisting *woof woof come too*

ORDINARY STRATA (LAKE SUPERIOR)

Glaciers pressed the sandstone cliffs

They made all this

How the grand lake mouths the land

The lake spells no thing

A child will be earth before their diapers are

"What did that man close the window about?"

A thousand plastic cars adrift

WINDOWS III

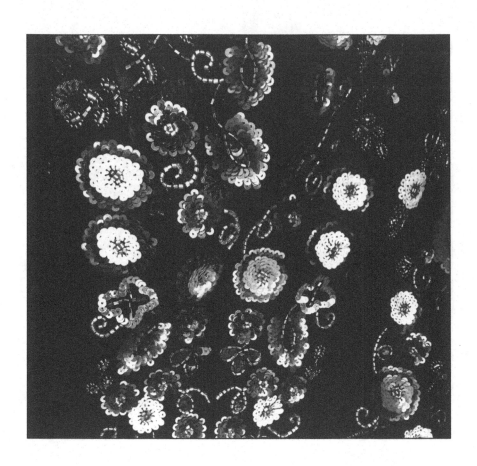

REPORT CARDS

late January 2020–early March 2020

ball ramp / rain

stick / bead

track / mood: happy /

snack /

spin

top / jack-in-the-box / musical

toys / open

and close drawers /

nap /

activities: keeping

hands to self / "stop

throwing" / mood: happy / apple / ate

lunch (some) / three

times wet /

touched (tenderly)

the cheeks of others

sleeping / woke

everyone else

up / mood: happy / *eeck*

eeck ack! / ah bah

bah bah! /

big grin / double

chin / activities: animal

sounds / held

spoon / ate

most but didn't like

the green

stuff / mood:

happy / finger

exercises / then following

simple commands

ORDINARY STRATA (CHICAGO)

Unfolds the week of weak storms

Tuesdays at ten an alarm sounds in the Midwest

Eager to suspend the end

The milk doesn't set

It's just water

Or Malört

A potential fern on the ridge of a shoulder

IT IS WITH A PATTERN AS WITH A FORTRESS

The waxy strip

peeled back discloses a patterned sticker meant

for pressing gently

to the wall's dull skin while smoothing

out each irksome

wrinkle by hand (a thumb for precision

along flawed edges—

palms for flattening vast fields of budding

bubbles) the goal

being to line the sliced side of

a lavender or

grass-green leaf's edge with the brink of

the next such

that one wall of the underused upstairs

bedroom blooms into

a tranquil space—aquatic maybe—underwater woodland

scene or site

of several bright watery gems—an enchanted

backdrop that could

only balance (it seems) the other objects

present: a *Moby-Dick*

board book whale mobile and pink Himalayan

salt lamp supposed

to—so claims O—expel negative ions

into the air—

a kind of lung care you'd never

have thought of…

This fashionable modern online-orderable boutique wallpaper arrives

in sticky ribbons

that can be removed with minimal effort

when one's (inevitably

someday) sick of the pattern their old

self picked unlike

the enduring glued designs still observable in

many a grandmother's

home or most of those that line

this Cleveland Heights

road replete with hundred-year-old "charms" as evidence

of another generation's

domestic "character"　　　　　The pattern before you is

purple lime blue

periwinkle and navy creating a vertiginous dizzying

effect (one might

claim *psychedelic*) when accumulated en masse causing

you to recall

all at once the sweet small child

who materialized unbidden

in your dream last night and wonder

if this kid—

(whose name was "Winter" like the current

season)—would enjoy

a similar image to contemplate each evening

before plummeting into

his own private slumber… (But wait—dream

children aren't real—

right?—unless they're a vision?) One should

remain open to

strange repetitions Strange repetitions like when last

week you found

yourself mesmerized not by the nursery's wall

but a small

room of William Morris florals tucked into

the center of

Cleveland's steamy (in a blizzard) free art

museum—Morris's show

showing that a single vine carefully rendered

can occur again

and again (and again) (and again) in

what one imagines

must be a text—or textile's—new

context but really

it isn't   It's just the same shape

re-seen and you

are by now (which is actually *then*)

a little different—

but by *now's* now you know the

image clearer or

at least with clarifying bewilderment—eyes scanning

inked pattern in

search of variance—minor mark or error—

tear—tremor—any

sign that the artist's hand can't draw

flawlessly the exact

petal twice (thrice) (forever)   It turns out

of course he

didn't   Morris printed—made templates preventing haphazard

traces of impatience

in the wooden block's precise pressure on

layers of etched

leaves—the leaves relying on accurate color

matches stamped in

the correct sections—connecting each stem's bend

to the next

in a series—the series prioritizing no

individual form but

instead the strength of a group's union

like—for example—

a Bruegel might—every citizen as irrefutably

relevant to a

bucolic tableau's panorama as their neighbor is

Some of Morris's

prints became wallpaper   Others are represented in

the deliberately mismatched

outfits of hipsters or on the adorable

(boring) front of

a newborn's romper because in infant fashion

all patterns are

perfect—perfect as a baby learning one

sound (*da da*

da da da) before the whole word

(world) comes stumbling

out   At your shower you received wraps

blankets bags and

onesies with a single printed image (skull

boat star or

fern) reproduced over and over again (*ugh*—

why are breeders

so *derivative*?) forecasting the inevitable truth that

soon your days

too will ensue such that the same

thing happens at

the exact same time—like a predictable

rhyme: pleasing sans

any surprise—the goal being to generate

a collaborative sequence

of habits that feel organic—a way

of behaving consistently

that's also thrilling?—like one who plates

painted flowers in

the same way—day after day—or

measures lines in

units of threes and sevens to reflect

the age at

which they first became the author of

another (a mother)

as if math could secure a sounder

path—as if

a poem broken open could sufficiently reveal

the circumstances of

the rowdy doubting mind that wrote it

like the rings

of an ancient pine or the stamped

itty bitty lines

of a new fingerprint's signature   The image

of vines and birds—strawberries and thorns—

sketched from sight

on site—like Morris's—are unlike how

you came to

know of honeysuckle marigold peacock or ivy

which was primarily

through the corporate mass production of pastoral

patterns in fashion

as now Winter will learn of his

namesake via hearsay

and research—stories of six-foot snow drifts—

illustrations of ice

floes on plastic bottles—capitalist tragedies—rumors

of the moods

of the coolest polar vortexes via literature

and experimental film

(or his parents' whims)—Winter (not yet

in existence)—will

soon snooze to the low drone of

a white noise

machine's subtle lullabye as opposed to the

messy orchestral cacophony

of backyard crickets—sonic density growing scarce—

sound scales muting—

the strata's data demonstrating abnormality's prominence over

previously reliable historical

pattern...   But don't wreck this room (yet)

with prediction   Just

        let's stare without purpose at the pattern

for a minute

Let's stare without purpose at the pattern

        for a minute

           Let's stare without purpose at the pattern

                for a minute

Let's stare without purpose at the pattern

        for a minute

ORDINARY STRATA (CLEVELAND)

Rotting meat silver lemon candlestick wax

Pleasure just out of reach

Sign up at the broken link

The first frame should set in motion a theme

Crafted to exist out of context

The vitriol of our age

Garbage obscene

ORDINARY STRATA (LAMBERTON ROAD)

Chimney too old and corroded to be usable

They told her "don't let it go to your head"

Egg sandwich with tomatoes and cheddar

Looking through an archway at the angle of a window

Satchel snoring on the kitchen rug

What is it possible to pause for

Inquiry of interruption

.

PHOTO CREDITS

Windows I

"Cleveland Lakefront" 1910. Cleveland Public Library, Cleveland Picture
Collection. Public Domain. https://cplorg.contentdm.oclc.org/
digital/collection/p4014coll18/id/942/rec/55

Morris, William. "Strawberry Thief." c. 1936. The Cleveland Museum of
Art. Gift of Mrs. Henry Chisholm. https://www.clevelandart.org/
art/1937.696.

Pagel, Caryl. "Report Card." 2020.

Pagel, Caryl. "Lakeview Cemetery Window." 2016.

Windows II

Pagel, Caryl. "Desk Pineapple." 2021.

Pagel, Caryl. "O's Hand." 2021.

Pagel, Caryl. "Garbage." 2021.

Pagel, Caryl. "Observatory." 2016.

Pagel, Caryl. "Ultrasound." 2018.

Windows III

Pagel, Caryl. "Wood Road." 2015.

Pagel, Caryl. "Dress Flowers." 2017.

Fischer, Carrie. "The Helping Hand." 2018. Palmer Square Park,
Chicago. Photo by Caryl Pagel. http://www.chicagotreeproject.org/
trees-2/carrie-fischer/.

Pagel, Caryl. "IHOP, Severance Center." 2015.

ACKNOWLEDGMENTS

Poems from this collection have appeared in various versions at the journals below; thank you to the editors.

Action, Spectacle: "Ordinary Strata (Cleveland)" x 5

ALL Review: "Ordinary Strata (Lamberton Road)," reprint

Apartment Poetry: "Severance Center" (originally titled "Séance")

Conduit: "Notes on *Notes on Thought and Vision*"

Denver Quarterly: "Ordinary Strata (Appledore Island)," "Ordinary Strata (Lamberton Road)," and "Ordinary Strata (Lake Erie)"

echoverse: "Ordinary Strata (Coventry)," "Ordinary Strata (Lamberton Road)," and "Ordinary Strata (Cottage Grove)"

Jellyfish Review: "It Is with A Pattern as With A Fortress"

The Mississippi Review: "The Vanitas Fly"

New American Writing: "Wilderness"

The Journal Petra: "A History of the Color Orange"

The Paris Review: "Saturday"

Windfall Room: "Ordinary Strata (Lake Erie)," audio version

Thank you to Alyssa Perry, Zach Savich, and Hilary Plum for reading. Thank you to Dorothy and John Fernanado for your report cards and your care. Thank you to Ossian Foley, Winter Foley, and the Pagels for your love.

Thank you to Stacy Szymaszek, Michelle Taransky, and Nikki Wallschlaeger for your kind words. Thank you to Ron Barron for the cover image, *Fall Nocturne*, 2015.

Thank you to Mary Biddinger, Amy Freels, Thea Ledendecker, Jon Miller, and everyone at The University of Akron Press for making beautiful books. Thank you to the Hermitage Artist Retreat. Thank you to my colleagues and students at Cleveland State University and in the NEOMFA program, particularly the students in my fall 2018 Craft & Theory course: "Ecopoetics, Connection, Compost, Deep Time, Unconformity, & Heat."

Caryl Pagel is the author of two previous books of poetry, *Twice Told* and *Experiments I Should Like Tried at My Own Death*, as well as a collection of essays, *Out of Nowhere Into Nothing*. She is an editor and publisher at Rescue Press and the director of the Cleveland State University Poetry Center. Pagel teaches poetry and nonfiction at Cleveland State University and in the Northeast Ohio MFA program.